Grief Doesn't Do Math

Heather H. Burwell, M.Div.

WESTBOW
PRESS®
A DIVISION OF THOMAS NELSON
& ZONDERVAN

WestBow Press books may be ordered through booksellers or by contacting:

WestBow Press
A Division of Thomas Nelson & Zondervan
1663 Liberty Drive
Bloomington, IN 47403
www.westbowpress.com
844-714-3454

ISBN: 978-1-6642-4469-6 (sc)
ISBN: 978-1-6642-4468-9 (e)

Library of Congress Control Number: 2021918480

Print information available on the last page.

WestBow Press rev. date: 10/20/2021

dedicated to family

acknowledgements

Thank you sincerely to the Hollands, Heltons, and Burwells for your ongoing, considerate love and support. Life is not easy, but you sure provide a shoulder to drive on when the winding, unyielding road gets treacherous. To Jerry Crutchfield, for believing in every creative effort I've ever forged full-throttle into, head and heart first. To Brenda McClearen, for her wisdom, and for informing me about Malinda Just, editor extraordinaire. To Malinda Just, for her careful and thoughtful, meaningful, timely work getting these words "just right." I don't have enough thank-yous for taking on this project. To Professor Bonnie Miller-McLemore who navigated a path for me through graduate school, and to her and Professor Graham Reside for suggesting this master's thesis expand into book format. To Lewis for giving our hearts a safe, loving home. You are our lighthouse and captain. To Mom for the gift of warmth and hospitality, for inviting everyone into her life to simply show extravagant love. To Dave for every second, every exchange, every moment we had on life's journey. Lastly, to a really incredibly sweet, creative, funny, compassionate, bright-eyed twelve year old, Jude. Kid ... you got it. You got the best of your Dad. Your heart will take you anywhere you want and need to go in this life. You're a natural, Jude.

author foreword

Hello, Dear Reader! Thank you for joining me on this walk. Let's not run, OK? Let's take this slow as the mountains in the distance unfold. What's our rush? Let's travel this path together with open hearts, willing to receive whatever may come. Let's also promise to utilize radical acceptance in the rainbow of emotions that will potentially arise. In this book, I am including journal entries, poems, and reflections over the course of seven years. This is my grief virgin voyage, and I share with you for a sole reason: to help other people sitting in their dinghies in torrential rainstorms, tossed upon similar waves. "… to whom much has been given, much will be required."[1] I've been given much pain, and feel it's my duty and honor to send forth the manner in which I survived so others might feel strengthened. It's not lip service; I really feel a conviction to help. As a chaplain, I would say I reside in the pain of others. This might sound awful, but actually, it's very rewarding. However, I might not say such a thing had I not been through my own pain path. After all, if you don't know the route, how can you help someone else down that road? If someone said, "I ran the New York Marathon," and you asked what it was like, you'd expect a pretty sure answer of the streets, turns, and hills. That's what I want to do—help the grief runners get through the marathon of pain that life will at some point throw at us, because eventually we'll all be hit with a loss landmine. While no one's

---

[1] Luke 12:48 (NRS).

journey is identical, my hope is that someone, even one person, can identify with something that provides them some measure of solace, even one teaspoon's worth. Teaspoons, while tiny and seemingly insignificant, add up to gallons over time. And I'm the first to say, in my view, time doesn't necessarily heal wounds. But my hope is that multiple teaspoons of light become a wide, deep vat of hope for you.

I thought it important to do this in a non-linear way to drive home my opinion that grief is no linear beast. Thus, the entries leapfrog from year to year, in no discernible order or arrangement. The frenetic-ness, the disorderliness, is perhaps the key ingredient to grief. This is no well-appointed dinner table with places for things and everything just so. No, the tablecloth was ripped out, Houdini-like, with smashing plates and crashing crystal, clanging forks and knives. What's left is a grand, hot, tornadic, unkind mess. Regardless of how it happened, what happened, or why it happened, the grave loss has occurred, and without our consent. No phone calls or texts or DMs about preparing to face the unfaceable. B.G. (Before Grief) is a thing of yesteryear; A.G. (After Grief) is the new kid on the block who isn't moving away anytime soon … perhaps never.

I am intentionally choosing to use my pain for a greater good because people in pain want and crave assurance they are okay. Then they need a heavy dose of reassurance. What they don't need is a guilt trip for not moving through someone else's inscribed stages of grief. People want to be affirmed and reaffirmed that, while all may not be well now, they are functioning. Functioning is enough some days when under the rule of grief. Getting out of bed is enough some days, and some days it is enough to rest in bed all day, feeling the typhoon. There is no prescription for how to do it. No RX pad can solve your pain or my pain, and no doctor can fix it.

As a griever, I have suffered and struggled immensely. As the mother to a grieving child, I have attempted to bear his immense loss of a father, all the while realizing my limits. As a chaplain, I sit with those individuals pressed down firmly, cemented in the mire and murkiness of grief. I try to provide comfort, emotional warmth, and compassionate presence. I rarely have answers for their pleading questions, but I sit with them inside the space of questions. I envision us, in my mind's eye, together in a clear bubble covered in question marks. One might think "the chaplain should have all the answers." In fact, patients have begged me for the solutions to why they suffer so. I cover this dilemma in my previous book, *Undeniable Presence: I Don't Know Where God is Not*. My humble answer to those searching for the painful whys is a sobering, yet bluntly honest, "I don't know."

As I asked individuals their thoughts on grief, an unplanned, seismic, hugely altering wave came upon this work! It turns out that grief is not only death-related, but also extends to the living. Many eager folks sent me their thoughts on grief, which exist on a spectrum of lost relationships at one end to the loss of beloved pets at the other and encompass the heart-wrenching grief that accompanies infertility and the grief of lost dreams. I implored if they would be willing to share their reflections. Resoundingly, each person was inclined to tell their personal story. To them I am forever grateful. While this redirected the book on a different and unexpected route than I had originally intended, it was meant to be. The voices of many are necessary to exhibit just how widespread the grief process is, and the myriad of shapes grief can and does take. As a chaplain, honoring others' stories is paramount. Empathy is being able to listen to another's truth while silently imagining how that would feel were it you. I appreciate you taking their words to heart, honoring their paths, and holding space for these truths.

I sincerely hope this book serves you in some capacity. My wish is that you will find some soul resonation, if even only one or two lines. If you have loved ones in the throes of grief, perhaps something inside these pages will provide some sort of salve for you to extend. I don't intend to erase or minimize anyone's grief. I do know for certain that what we don't talk about festers and creates havoc in our personhood and the lives of those we love. What I seek to do is share, and in that sharing, normalize the fact that loss and grief are the great equalizer of all of our lives. So, with that being said, let's dust the world off our shoulders, unplug, and dig our heels in. Welcome.

part one

the garment

Is there a way for a human being to be encapsulated into a sleeve of inky darkness? I mean, entirely … skin, bones, cells, cartilage, muscle, and spirit? Can all of these constitute a desolate expanse of sheer despair? As calamitous as it sounds, it is oh so much worse to be the subject, the one slipping into the casing, but not trying it on for size, garbing oneself in an unremovable suit. This attire is meant for keeps, for life unto death, from daylight to damp grave.

This is how it goes. The garment as it were is draped across an antique rose velvet chaise lounge, no pilings or shredding threads hanging to and fro. It is runway-ready and pristine, dangerously still, lying in wait and weight. Phenomenally it possesses the innate ability to be one size fits all. Fat, thin, short, tall, gut, six-pack abs, aged gray man or young spry child … no matter. It will definitely fit, and like a glove. There is a tiny white tag attached by a black thread that simply reads: For You. There is no 'From' information because by the time it covers you, the sender's identity is known. But when it is slipping onto your essence, it is crystalline clear from your epidermis through to your aorta like a bar-room dart …

Someone you love is gone.

The floor is all I see. Creamy tiles soaked in tear waves are subservient to my eyes morphing and folding into each miniscule concave, under me now in the guest bathroom. My April-spring-dirt brown hair is salty and stringy wet. It actually lays quite pretty against the white and gray contradiction, in a flash, I decide. But pretty is not what is acquirable today. My clothes are strewn as I look around my body on all fours. Under my right arm, skinny jeans and faded cotton underwear rumpled up in the back corner. To my left, mini mountains of dust screaming for attention. Glance to my middle, my shirt hanging onto my body like I am to my heart. This bathroom is tiny. I'm sandwiched between the pedestal sink and old beautiful white cast iron tub and this is okay because this is the house I love. That vomit looks pinkish … blood? Kool-Aid? Beets from my smoothies? When the baby opens the wood door, it will hit me straight in the head. But that is not now's worry. His daddy has just died.

How will I tell him? How will I tell me, much less him? How can I be a good mother and break this baby's heart that daddy is gone? Is my heart actually breaking in this bathroom? I feel internal shattering, heat waves behind my ribcage. God forbid I have a heart attack in here and leave him totally alone in this world. He's out there in his playroom doing what the room implies. He's clicking his Thomas the Trains on the train table, doing his daily joy. I hear his sweet chatter and the clangs of train whistles from his toys. We just helped him break his pacifier not so long ago it seems. He is such a big boy, potty-trained, sleeping in his room without rails on his bed. Soon he will toddle toward this door with his precious knees in his play clothes and knock, calling out "Mama?" And what will this mama do then? I'm terrified of destroying his heart with this fatal news. He's so purely angelic, innocent, blue-eyed and true. How could I possibly tell him anything bad? Something that will rearrange his core, send his heart into something wider and deeper and scarier than the North Atlantic Ocean? What kind of good mother does that? I cannot save him from this unfair, rotten reality. I have to be honest with him, there is no other way. But how? He was just playing with him hours ago, back when the world was beautiful. The sinkhole came so unbelievably quick, so frighteningly fast, like a cold snap. The sun flipped to a moonless, starless sky in a single eye-blink. What are the words I use from my mouth to tell him his daddy is gone and will not be coming back?

a child's view of grief

◦~

*Just so, grief doesn't come and go. Our world has a lot
of grief. Sometimes not. But life is only here if God
is here. Grief is a thing … not a feeling. Many times
this is mistaken by. Not everyone has grief.*

- JUDE, AGE EIGHT

the problem with
grief stages

⌒ℳ⌒

Undoubtedly there are landmark movements on the stages of grief—with Elisabeth Kübler-Ross' infamous five stages sustaining the most prodigious prominence.[2] The millions of individuals who have obtained substantial alleviation from the grief-staging approach can attest to its countless benefits. This book's purpose is to bring into question the grief stages concept, while recognizing its potential as a healing balm. This objective observation is, if you will, for people who, like me, could not work a linear path along grief's sojourn. After my husband passed away, I found myself in all, or various parts, of the stages simultaneously over a half-decade's span. Our son, who was age four at the time, has endured his own harrowing grief experience with the acceptance piece appearing futile. As a chaplain, I have had the joy of listening to others' life stories. A patient named Carol, whilst discussing her husband's death, poignantly labeled her grief journey a "five-year fog." This fog is precisely why the five stages are conceivably lacking in efficiency and meaning.

When presented with a topic of our choosing for Vanderbilt Divinity School's master's senior project, I immediately knew which direction to go. As one absorbing her own grief journey,

---

[2] Elisabeth Kübler-Ross, *On Death and Dying* (New York: Simon & Schuster, 1969).

and simultaneously assisting a young child with his, the subject of grief was a real-life, heavily highlighted topic. In a pastoral care course, a discussion arose upon the lack of personal memoirs on grief. From the assigned texts, it seemed there were plenty of well-versed scholars and psychologists able to instruct on the grieving process. The portion that seemed to be missing was a personal narrative, a sincere truth-telling, combined with careful analysis and reconstruction. For me, it was imperative to include journal entries that reflect bottom-floor grief in this book's analysis. Also crucial was the inclusion of my son's quotes, as I find a child's view of grief essential and heartfelt. As a creative writer, this lack of grief memoir lit a fire within me, to create such a text of honesty, grit, and truth that also works on constructive proposals beyond the five stages.

That being said, the five stages are now ingrained into the paradigm of human consciousness. Of the stages, pastoral theologian Bonnie Miller-McLemore reveals, "Not only have they permeated the professional world of the hospital, they have also shaped attitudes and oriented the thinking of the general public."[3] While clanging a resounding gong of inquiry into the five stages is a daunting task, it is well worth an in-depth perusal. Lamentably, the loss of loved ones is a certainty. We will all be grievers at some point in our lives. This inevitability is precisely the reason for this book: to find additional, alternative grieving methods.

The "what stage are you in?" query plummets heavily upon conflicted ears. A byproduct of said systematic approach can be a sense of failure or loss of autonomy. Of Kübler-Ross' approach, Dutch clinical psychologists Margaret Stroebe and Henk Schut, with Boston gerontologist Kathrin Boerner assert: "Furthermore, bereaved people stand to benefit from her compassionate, easily

---

[3] Bonnie J. Miller-McLemore, *Death, Sin and the Moral Life* (Atlanta: Scholars, 1988), 95.

accessible writing and teaching. However, such merits are on a completely different level from evaluation of the actual stages; it does not follow that the stages are adequate representations of what grieving people go through."[4] Sufferers of loss need foundational, non-judgmental support along their personal journeys, not a list of expectations demanding adherence. Kübler-Ross reveals, "The five stages, denial, anger, bargaining, depression, and acceptance are a part of the framework that makes up our learning to live with the one we lost."[5] But could that very framework be constrictive, corralling grievers into an unhelpful cage? Interestingly, Kübler-Ross also infers that this is not an orderly system, but a mere recommendation, when she states, "They are tools to help us frame and identify what we may be feeling. But they are not stops on some linear timeline in grief."[6] Yet, in actuality, many individuals ascertain this process as explicitly linear in nature, starting with shock and ending in acceptance. To solidify this argument, "The first four stages contain negative and potentially destructive emotions if not forsaken in order to reach the final stage of acceptance," reveals Miller-McLemore.[7] Multiple scholars and studies have disputed Kübler-Ross' claims of innocent staging processes. One such theologian, Roy Branson, concludes this as Kübler-Ross' only means of conceptualization.[8] Therefore, whilst intentional or coincidental, the fact remains that there is indeed a sequential nature of the five stages.

Kübler-Ross' groundbreaking work evolved during her tenure

---

[4] Margaret Stroebe, Henk Schut, and Kathrin Boerner, "Cautioning Health-Care Professionals: Bereaved Persons Are Misguided Through the Stages of Grief." OMEGA 74 (2017): 455–473. https://journals. sagepub. com/doi/pdf/10.1177/0030222817691870 (accessed October 14, 2019).

[5] Elisabeth Kübler-Ross and David Kessler, *On Grief and Grieving* (New York: Scribner, 2005), 7.

[6] Ibid., 7.

[7] Miller-McLemore, 95.

[8] Ibid., 95.

as a psychiatrist during the 1960s and the 1970s. "Her work has been so integrated into death care that medicine has forgotten that her points once needed to be argued. Her stage theory is no longer understood as a theory of the dying process, but rather as the dying process itself,"[9] reveals theologian Richard Coble. Kübler-Ross formulated a path for dying patients to discover resolve and peace. Within her psychological studies, she developed a profound interest in near death experiences. Thus, the impetus for her work was caring for the actively dying, and not specifically the grieving. Somewhere along the way individuals began adapting this to myriad scenarios of life transitions. Unfortunately, those who had lost loved ones were akin to sitting ducks, desperate for any information on post-loss healing. Therefore, it is my personal belief that the five stages were absorbed by, and re-routed onto, the grieving community out of sheer need.

This yearning of humanity for healing from grief created the co-opting of the five stages onto grievers worldwide. By taking a closer look, it is intriguing to note the difference in how two individuals, one dying and one grieving, could interpret these stages. Denial, anger, bargaining, depression, and acceptance are the ordered phases. Herein is where the problem originates. Denial, for example, is not an absolute nor a definite. In chaplaincy settings, I have seen firsthand that many do not experience denial whatsoever. It is my experience that such individuals have either known such an event was likely on their horizon, or they possess a deep, abiding faith that makes them unshakable. There are no allowances for these scenarios on the spectrum of the five stages. In addition, a griever may have been mentally and emotionally prepared for such loss that makes denial an impossibility. With this, it is evident that there are already issues arising from the initiation of the stages within the grief paradigm. These processes

---

[9] Richard Coble, *The Chaplain's Presence and Medical Power* (Lanham: Lexington, 2018), 122–123.

of life cannot be reduced to emotional psyches across the board of all humanity for all time. Within the lifespans of complex individuals, there are too many variables at play to employ a timeline of expectations.

Stage theory is the psychological and sociological term to describe orderly processes. Three professors in the Netherlands and Boston developed a critique of Kübler-Ross' stage theory as it pertains to grief. They insist, "As we show, the stage theory of grief falls short ... There is no scientific foundation, and decades of research have shown that most people do not grieve in stages. Using stages as a guide in work with bereaved is unhelpful and may even cause harm."[10] If their claims ring true, then what is the draw of stage theory to the human mind? The professors assert, "The abiding appeal is perhaps its simplicity. In the midst of such emotional complexity as characterizes the bereavement experience, the stages offer something to hold on to, both descriptively and prescriptively."[11] In other words, for grievers in overwhelming circumstances, the ease of "working a system" may feel helpful on the surface. Nevertheless, the professors conclude that the application of stage theory, when meted toward grief, "should be discarded by all concerned (including bereaved persons themselves); at best, it should be relegated to the realms of history."[12] This suggestion that the five stages deserve eradication is profound.

In my journey, I found myself overwhelmed with expectations. The curiosity arose in my own personhood that perhaps the five stages are a vehicle of projection. With this complicit theory now streaming into the consciousness of humanity, maybe we all expect each other to progress quicker than what is possible. I shudder to recall a woman telling me "other women have gotten

---

[10] Stroebe, "Cautioning," 456.

[11] Ibid., 467.

[12] Ibid., 456.

over it." *It.* What she failed to comprehend is that one never gets over it. After the loss of David, I walked again to be sure, but I walked with a cumbersome limp, which I expect to engage the rest of my life. While social worker Judy Tatelbaum would likely describe my station as "unhealthy"[13] and "pathological grief,"[14] this is my experience to possess. Grief and loss become steady, faithful companions always present and at the ready. Hence, there is no ability for a be-all, end-all overcoming concept. And such a suggestion is a silly pipe dream.

Over our grief journey as mother and son, we have never once questioned one another regarding our feelings (or stages). We accept each other's place in the moment, often reflective, often somber, always disappointed. Never would I place upon my son any sort of numbered system, or grief proficiency test to ace. This is not because I doubt his abilities; I would not do so because that is overwhelmingly non-compassionate. Therefore, why would I dare expect this of myself? Self-compassion has to be an all-encompassing trait of grief, particularly when surrounded by and immersed in the projection of others' assumptions. Self-care needs to be an active component as well. Thus, if I'm exercising twofold compassion and care for self, any approach that infringes upon such calls for deconstruction, or at the very least, a critical inquiry.

The narratives of individuals I've encountered in chaplaincy ministry are resoundingly similar. Greta and Paul, who lost their son in a car accident seven years prior, related, "Everyone says it [the loss] fades in time, but we've found just the opposite. With Kevin's death, the time stretches beyond itself, if that makes sense. We miss him more each passing year." This phenomena, this time dysfunction, reverberates with me; it certainly feels that the loss is actually increasing over time, as if our departed have

---

[13] Judy Tatelbaum, *The Courage to Grieve* (New York: Harper, 1980), 49.
[14] Ibid., 49.

taken the clocks to their graves. Time has a different slant for the grieving. The grotesque, swirling fog is at once confounding and confusing. The aforementioned Carol explicitly confirmed that the five-year fog was a mixture of sadness and anger. She said it with such intensity that I inherently sensed acceptance was a distant mountain for her, too. How could we really get over people we've loved? It is my belief that is such an impossibility that placing any sort of program upon loss is moot and ill-fated. When a loved one is gone, the ground shifts and fractures completely and eternally. As C.S. Lewis inquired in his honest reflection on grief after the death of his wife whom he met late in his life, "Did you ever know, dear, how much you took away with you when you left?"[15] What—and who—is gone cannot be replaced.

---

[15] C.S. Lewis, *A Grief Observed* (New York: HarperCollins, 1996), 61.

j o u r n a l

It's been three years and five days, four hours, and forty-five minutes. Or is it five minutes? The sun attempts to peek out and give me some desperately needed hope-shine, but the clouds are chuckling back in full-on cover mode. I can plainly see that those allegedly helpful five stages of grief are insufficient, damaging, and making me feel inadequate. My convoluted grief traverse actually began with acceptance, (what?) which is bizarre and backward. I hit the last stage first! I guess Elisabeth Kübler-Ross would give me a hearty and well-deserved F minus. In reflection, it is painfully obvious. My social media posts were oozing in positivity and hope just one day after you died. I pontificated on how fortunate we were to have you the short time we did and carried on and on about the glories of reuniting with you one day in heaven. Gross. Not normal. It's one thing to gird up your loins and be all Jackie Kennedy about it all, with stern lip and brave face for the kids. It's quite another to throw on rose-colored glasses and tell the world about my newfound acceptance at a time I shouldn't have. What was I thinking? Literally ... what thoughts were taking up residence inside my battered pain-brain? Little Mrs. Sunshine was full-force optimism hours after her beloved passed? No, that's not even a characteristic I would possess on a good, normal day. Where's my shock? Did that all somehow fall in a shock box and seal itself away from me in the span of a day? Does Mama Bear mode, fending for her child, send me beyond the first necessary (so I hear) stage of shock? I'm not grieving right, and it is evident to me I never have. C. S. Lewis, in all of his theological brilliance, apparently couldn't grieve right either. In *A Grief Observed*, he said, "For in grief nothing 'stays put,' One keeps on emerging from a phase, but it always recurs." This process is a swirling tornado with eyes everywhere; there is no nucleus. How lovely it would be just to wring my hands of the pain and sail away, abandoning it to the wind. I am such an ineffective griever. I don't do it right. What am I supposed to do?

Lance's Experience

"Ignored Grief Doesn't Go Away"

When I was eight months old, my father never came home. He was tragically killed in an automobile accident after a late work call as he was trying to support my family. It took me thirty-eight years to actually acknowledge that he was real to me, and that he loved me with all of his heart.

My situation was blessed in many ways, one of which is that my mom was able to find an amazing man, who adopted me and married her. He became my dad before I was two years old. I've been so blessed to have him as a loving father and a wonderful provider for my mom and me. That was part of the problem. Having no memory of my birth father, I can now see as I look back, that I never even acknowledged his existence. My mom at times would attempt to sit me down and go through his old belongings, but I think I learned at an early age to "build a wall" to his existence.

I had a set story I would share anytime someone would realize that my dad had died when I was young. I immediately would answer "Yes, but I'm so lucky, I don't remember him and have had a great dad." There was an issue with this. I was still blocking the fact that he was real to me, that he ever existed. It messed me up much more than I realized.

I was a shy, only child. When my mom had tried to go

through his old stuff, I had that wall built. I had no interest. I now see that it was because I had guilt of acknowledging someone I didn't remember. It felt wrong to acknowledge my dead father as it might hurt my 'dad' that I know. There were times that we had to attend a funeral in Memphis where he was buried, and my mom would walk me to his grave and stop to show me. Once again, I had such a wall of protection built, that I had zero interest. It was just another grave, like the thousands of others in the graveyard. I felt zero emotion!

I felt I was managing life the best I could, and having no recollection of him with no memory of his voice or anything. I thought it wasn't a big deal. His pictures were not displayed and he was never really discussed. Out of sight, out of mind! I realize now that if I acknowledged my father, it felt like 'cheating' on the only dad I had ever known.

Life progressed and as I was never very popular or confident in myself, I can look back and see how this grief weighed on my soul even though I didn't realize it. But it made the loss much easier to ignore because I had no memory. And I sure didn't want to hurt the only dad I remembered by even attempting to give love to the one I didn't recall.

Another thing I didn't realize until I had healed is that I hated when my mom would cry! And she was one who would cry at a *Little House on the Prairie* episode, among other things, but she also would cry when she was proud of me. I hated this and I didn't know why. I hated it so much that I built a wall with her, too. Even in adulthood, when I was experiencing great success, I would not tell her because I didn't want her to cry. As I began to heal, I learned that when I was a baby after my dad died, she would drive me around and just sob uncontrollably. Wow, no wonder. And this shows how unresolved grief impacts us on a subconscious level.

Unresolved grief can impact so many relationships in our lives. We can try to sweep it under the rug, ignore it, but it doesn't make grief go away—not even close. Life forced me to get out of my pain, to grow and prosper, but it was always there lurking, just below the surface.

When I was thirty-eight, I was talking to a close friend who realized how much of a burden this was on my life. No one had really forced the issue with me until that moment. My friend had the necessary care, courage and love to ask me a question that no one else had asked me: "Do you not realize, you were the last thought on his mind, that he loved you with all of his heart?" I had never allowed myself to consider this truth, and at that moment my life changed! I was in my front yard, late at night, and for the first time in my life, I looked to the sky and I uttered aloud, tears streaming down my face, "Dad I Love You!" I didn't just utter it, I felt it! At that moment, that release, I saw a green shooting star cross the sky, I had no doubt that was his reply to me! I knew in that moment that he did love me, that he has always loved me, and had patiently waited for me to give him that love back. It was one of the most freeing moments of my life!

After that moment of release, I began to accept my father who had passed almost forty years earlier to be a part of my daily life. He was showing me he was still there to love me! It taught me a lesson. I don't know what happens after we die, but I know that those who pass on do not go far! They are still "out there." I began to incorporate him into my life and went through this stuff voluntarily. I had pictures of him in my world for the first time ever. I began to talk to him regularly when I felt I needed his love. And I would often see that green shooting star the more I did!

Due to this release, I have been able to love my dad now so much more freely. There was no more competition, a feeling that I can only love one. I am so blessed to have two amazing fathers, one who is still living, one who is there more and more for me in his own way.

I have seen more of the green shooting stars, so many other signs that he is still there for me. I am so lucky to have two dads, and to be able to fully love them both. It is one of the most freeing things I've ever experienced. You cannot sweep grief under the rug. There isn't a rug big enough.

I am still working to find my calling in life, I am facing a lot of challenges every day that I never thought I would have to face, but I know that I have two dads who still love me and are there for me. And once I opened this door to grief—to healing—I have found some timeless lessons just by going through my dad's old stuff. Be it a book, an inspirational typing or cassette tape, I feel more and more that I am supposed to carry on my birth father's message that he never got to fulfill!

Sharon's Experience

I have grief around "would have been" times. My brother died when he was fourteen and I was twelve. You have the initial grief and loss, but then you have a lifetime of those "would have", "should have", and "wonder" moments. He would have been graduating. He would have been getting a job, getting married, becoming an uncle. He should have been at my wedding, he should be here for holidays, to help with aging parents, to see my daughter grow up. I wonder what he would be like, what his career would be, what he would think about xyz … The thing I have learned in the past twenty-five years is that we tend to think of grief as a stage, or a state, something fleeting. But it is so much more than that—it permeates everything and becomes a very real, defining, and familiar part of who you are. And, you never really get away from its impact on you—"Oh, you're an only child, so you don't get it." "Where do your siblings live?" Everyone has their own version of the harmless comments and conversation starters that happen all the time. I often find myself evading the truth simply not to make the other person feel bad or awkward. I never realized how deeply and constantly his death would impact me in my everyday life, even if it's not from feelings of sadness or grief in the moment, just everyday stuff.

Beverly's Experience

Life and death go together. I know many people never think of death ... they pretend like it does not exist. But, death is a season in life. We have to live with an expectation that losses will be part of life. Life is to be valued. We are not promised tomorrow. I think part of grieving well is being prepared for losses and being able to build new relationships and dreams once chapters end. I have a dear family member who lost her mother (she was in her late 90s). She had never allowed herself to consider or think about life without her mother. The way we think about life and death greatly impacts our ability to process death.

part two

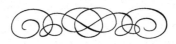

what the birds know

"Show her the birds!" he exclaims in a midnight dream in vivid technicolor. He and I are standing under pterodactyl-sized white birds gliding, mind you, not flapping. I am uncertain of the species. Our necks are craned upward to view this simple yet poignant sight of soaring creatures, wings fully outstretched, perhaps a span of ten feet. I can hear the soft whisper of the glide. They simply, yet majestically, soar. He is smiling from ear to ear, delighted to show me these birds. David has recently passed on at the young age of forty. I presume David is asking God to put on this show for me, to prove the beauty of Heaven, to ease my mind and bring me some piecemeal of peace, though a peace which I honestly do not remotely have at that moment in waking life. The birds are pristine and beautiful and I am in sincere awe at their glorious sight. I am in particular amazement that these birds need not flap their wings, relaying a message that in Heaven all is effortless, that perhaps there is no wind to strain against, to move against. All is calm, all is right. Winds are of the earth, sickness is of the earth. In Heaven, people are happy about showing others soaring birds. Upon waking and contemplating the dream, I try to reflect on all the Scriptures I was raised on and to bring to mind any regarding birds. My mind immediately directs to "not even a sparrow falls without God knowing" (Matthew 10:29). I recall the dove sent from the ark. I know that birds are prominent within Scripture. In literature, Thoreau remarked that a sparrow landing upon him was a profound experience.

David and I never discussed anything pertaining to birds in our relationship. We weren't bird-watchers or even remotely interested in the subject. We typically passed the bird exhibits at the zoos trying to reach the cages of something "more interesting" like giraffes and elephants. I've thought of this often; what is with the birds and why are they becoming seemingly telltale messengers? Is David able, as a remote figure from Heaven, choosing the feathers right now to send us hopeful signals that he is still very much alive and sees us? One can only hope. There is a very specific, linear trail of signals and communications he has left for our now nine-year old son and me. Jude says, "I think the feathers make us healthier." The feathers appear at least a few times a month, in random locales. One time I was trying to make a big decision, opened the back door, and a feather was lying on the threshold right at my feet. I met with a counselor a few weeks after his passing and the first thing I see on the wall is a pattern of white feathers wrapped around the wall behind her chair. Feathers. There they are again. It seems they are literally everywhere. I cannot escape them, not that I would want to.

The grief is so weighty and drowning and soul-soaking that I will take anything I can get. I am aware I could be inventing these signs in my mind, but it's all too surreal not to be something. I decide it has to mean something and be the working of some force beyond little old me. I need peace that he is at peace and if feathers are the means of divine communication, then I will gladly accept. Tiny downy feathers like the stuffing inside a pillow have fallen from above, landing before us, appeared resting on the floor in front of us, and randomly arrived from seemingly out of nowhere. I cannot count the times this has happened. When my son and I visited San Diego, he was running down the pier and turned to me with a massive white feather, so proud to show me. "Look, Mom!" We kept the feather. Another late afternoon, Jude was playing in the backyard. A feather fell from a tree or the sky, and he said, "Look a feather! That's Daddy saying hi to me!" He was full of delight at this discovery. What to make of these feathers? Do I believe in signs? Do I really believe it is possible that somehow David could be sending us feathers? Could he be? One day we were driving to visit his parents' home. We stopped at a traffic light in their hometown before some train tracks and about a million tiny white fluffs surrounded our car, like our own little private snowstorm. I was taken aback and told Jude, "Maybe that's Daddy." I don't know if the fluffs were from trees, from the weather, or from a higher place. We were covered over and it felt a lot like all-encompassing love. Jude and I were walking through our living room one morning and he looked down, spying two tiny downy-soft feathers, one for each of us. Jude was so excited; he put them in a special little box. Another morning, a robin was playing chase with him in the front yard. A feather floated in the air as the robin flew away. Jude said, "That black feather is from Daddy." What do the birds know? What do they see through their tiny eyes, orbs fronting bodies of feathers? We know they chirp, sing, fly, build nests and raise families. Can they possibly be modern-day messengers from those gone before us? Could they be used by angels to reach us with hope to encourage us? Plausible not. Logical not. But what I have seen causes me to believe birds have a purpose more than just flying. What I've borne witness to tells me they are guided to the suffering to deliver promises in things unseen. Why the bird? Their quantity and ease of dropping feathers make them ideal for message-delivery. Their ability to cover long distances via air also make them the perfect candidates. So we trust in the ways of the Creator of birds. We trust if the Most High wants us reassured with feathers, then that is more than able to happen. We have faith. And we cling tightly to our feathers that God has David in the shadow of His wings, and us, too.

a child's view of grief

Grief is like the Nationals beating the Astros in the World Series.
Grief comes out of nowhere, and it was very unexpected.
- JUDE, AGE TEN

grief reflections and refractions

⌒*ℳ*⌒

This project aspires to envision grief processes through a wider lens, reframed into a more compassionate process inclusive of personal grief journeys. I seek to find alternative avenues for grief with less strings attached. With the systemic, cultural aspects surrounding the impactful nature of the five stages, for the griever's best interest, various characteristics need to be addressed in order for meaningful change to occur. By unveiling the pushback from theological and psychological realms, a more comprehensive scope can be enacted. Additionally, and perhaps of greater value, the personal narratives of grievers affected by expectations take us to the heart of the matter. If the five stages of grief inflict any measure of harm upon grievers, what are alternative approaches for application? While dismantling damaging religious rhetoric and psychological language can surely be a daunting undertaking, grievers need solace in a less restrictive and non-linear manner than the five stages require. In order to eradicate such self-criticism, a gentler persuasion of grief is needed.

For further insight into strategies for healthier grieving, it is imperative to address the theological and socio-psychological aspects. The weight of the five stages in modern cultural consciousness cannot be overstated. The sources of said weight are deeply rooted and ingrained in multiple facets. For a theological study, I will begin with an in-depth look into the heart of Jesus. John reveals, "In the beginning was the Word..."[16] By initiating this study with the Word, and Christ in his perfect fullness, we unravel the grieving process from its origins.

One early Biblical reference points to Joseph observing a similar practice of sitting shiva, a prominent, modern practice within Judaism. The loved one's family members receive friends to celebrate and mourn the deceased. Genesis 50:10 reveals: "When they came to the threshing floor of Atad, which is beyond the Jordan, they held there a very great and sorrowful lamentation; and he observed a time of mourning for his father seven days" (NRSV). The Rabbis of the Talmud invoke Genesis 7:10 as a seven-day mourning period for Methuselah, a time that immediately preceded the Flood. To date, Judaism honors the dead and the living by intentional community without expectation of sequential stages. Judaism is renowned for timely, emotionally-efficient grieving practices. This is accomplished by the act of presence. The holy reverence arises from the communal custom of kinship as mourners do the simple yet profound act of sitting with the grieving. The power of presence is magnified via this verb, the action of sitting.

How did Jesus grieve? We do not see Jesus progress through any sort of sequential staging system. We visualize a human with the capacity to handle difficult emotions in a positive, healthy manner. According to Scripture, it is most notably recognized that "Jesus wept."[17] The interpretation in Greek is literally "Jesus shed tears." This is critical in displaying that Christ expressed personal anguish through the overt action of crying. He was not hesitant to convey grief, and in an open forum. In mourning the death of his beloved friend Lazarus, he simultaneously grieved with Lazarus' sisters, Mary and Martha, and lamented the reality

---

[16] John 1:1 (KJV).
[17] John 11:35 (KJV).

of death. Biographer Frank Mead relays, "It was a friendship born in heaven, meant for earth. Jesus and Lazarus, divine conspirators, friends of men, have made us friends with death."[18] Indeed, Jesus bemoaned the death of Lazarus while standing on the verge of lifting him from death to life. Still, even knowing the idyllic and redemptive end to come, Jesus shed tears of grief. "He knew the truth of the loss of his friend, but with a united heart he could see not just the truth of his loss, but the truth of his Father's love and plan. Jesus could see through to the resurrection."[19]

We also see Jesus' grief when he faces his own impending death. "And about the ninth hour Jesus cried with a loud voice, saying, Eli, Eli, lama sabachthani? that is to say, My God, my God, why hast thou forsaken me?"[20] Here we see Jesus overcome by his own grief, and his expression of the "anguish of being abandoned."[21] Jesus is at once experiencing multiple aspects of grief, including a sense of abandonment, of which "there are few things in life more painful."[22] As a man who lived and breathed, fully operating within the human experience, Jesus freely grieved. In their research on loss, pastoral theologians Kenneth Mitchell and Herbert Anderson assert, "We (as Christians) are more free to grieve precisely because our faith is grounded in the promise of a Presence from whom we cannot be separated."[23] The author of Matthew suggests that Jesus knew he would soon be beside his Father, yet still he endured an abiding, deep grief. His agony

---

[18] Frank Mead, *Who's Who in the Bible* (New York: Harper & Bros., 1934), 215.

[19] Barber, Betsy. "Grieving Like God," The Good Book (blog). Oct. 24, 2017. Accessed Oct. 12, 2019. https://www.biola.edu/blogs/good-book-blog/2017/grieving-like-god.

[20] Matthew 27:46, (KJV).

[21] Kenneth R. Mitchell and Herbert Anderson, *All Our Losses, All Our Griefs* (Louisville: Westminster John Knox, 1983), 69.

[22] Ibid., 69.

[23] Ibid., 102.

was raw and real. There was no adherence to societal expectations or stage theory. He simply, yet boldly, conveyed interior feelings in an outward display. We have much to learn from this fearless expression. If we as Christians are made in God's image, then grieving is a trait for us to replicate, not avoid. "When we grieve, we are being like Jesus," according to theologian Betsy Barber.[24] For the Christian, such moments of grief perceive the overarching truth of heaven. Our faith gives us foundational hope. We know the end of the story, and we know that it is good.

While Jesus did not shy away from vulnerability with open grief, some narratives within religion create further pain with ill-suited words. Certain narratives, particularly those in the religious realm, can be more damaging than redeeming. The phrases such as "God needed another angel" and "God never gives us more than we can handle" often fall upon bewildered ears. I recall a father, who upon hearing that his daughter had passed because "God needed another rose in His garden," sternly replied, "God is God. Can't He just make another rose instead of taking mine?" Well-meant expressions contain the ability to inflict additional anguish. The issue herein is that such narratives become part of the larger lexicon, which seeps into the mainstream. Said narratives seek to administer a bandage on another's grief by pacifying pain with token phrasing, likely with the best intentions. Rather than healing, however, such words can drive wounds deeper. "Assurances that the deceased is with God may set aside our anxiety about the future of someone we love, but they do not diminish our sense of loss," Mitchell and Anderson argue.[25] Oftentimes grievers prefer simple presence with others, and words are unnecessary. After his wife passed away, Clark, a young husband, stated, "The last thing I want to hear about is religion or God. Maybe one day ... but not now."

---

[24] Barber. "Grieving."
[25] Mitchell, 122.

After David's death, I heard many such phrases that hurt. The "God has a plan" sentence may indeed be true, but it can be unhelpful to hear inside the walls of the caverns of grief. Those four words echo like resounding shame to a griever: "Of course! I should know this and not be sad. Right?" This suggestion can invite a spiraling circle of shame onto the griever at a harrowing time. While critiquing her work with this project, Kübler-Ross convincingly and aptly asserts, "Once the patient dies, I find it cruel and inappropriate to speak of the love of God."[26] Words can inflict additional harm *or* vital healing. A patient, MaryAnn, who had recently lost her mother in a bizarre accident said to me, "I know there's a God, but I don't sense Him right now." Such expressions must be met with compassion and understanding. As chaplains, we must meet people where *they* are, not where we are. As humans, empathy is most helpful for connection. With sincere empathy, we can reach others and be reached as well.

Western attitudes of death are also at play. How would Jesus react to the harmful narrative "big boys don't cry" with the awareness that he himself openly wept, for all to see? Mitchell and Anderson point to the "Stoic argument that losing self-control is losing one's basic stance toward life. The Stoic must remain in control, since by definition grief is irrational and often uncontrollable."[27] While Stoicism is indeed a factor in secular culture, Miller-McLemore argues, "Christian consolation does not mean Stoic calm, indifference, or denial of passion. No one, even Christ, has the ability to achieve such forbearance."[28] Full expressions of grief are part and parcel of the grieving experience. To suggest removal of such expression is to neglect a mandatory process necessary for healing and recovery. Rather than remain bottled up within an individual, or placed on a spectrum, the

---

[26] Elisabeth Kübler-Ross, *On Death and Dying* (New York: Simon & Schuster, 1969), 183.

[27] Mitchell, 102.

[28] Miller-McLemore, 32.

gamut of emotions need to surface. By removing the exhortation of stages, a griever can mourn as they see fit.

To suggest a griever do the three-syllable yet arduous task of "moving on" is to imply such is in the realm of possibility. The answer lies not in what stage grievers find themselves, nor the potential stages worked through. The answer only rests in where the griever resides emotionally in that space of time. The imposition of any sort of linear process is non-compassionate and presumptuous. As a society we are inclined toward—even obsessed with—systematic, step-by-step formulas. We have been conditioned to take a list-based approach toward achievement. Look at how many books reveal the precise amount of numbers needed to overcome challenges or find success. We can conquer life's tsunami waves with convincing titles such as *"The Ten Amazing Steps to Success," "Twelve Steps to Greatness,"* or *"Seven Steps to Health."* For the residual impact it has had—not on the dying—but grieving, Kübler-Ross could have coined her book *"Five Steps to Overcoming Your Grief."* As stated, this mindset has resoundingly soaked into mainstream consciousness and is offered up to those experiencing various life changes. Divorce? You need the five stages. Job loss? Read about the five stages. House destroyed by fire? Simply work these five steps for ultimate healing. All life scenarios have been co-opted and corrupted to require a staging system in order for recovery. But, as we've uncovered, grief does not do math. Grief is not linear.

Interestingly, Kübler-Ross herself, upon later reflection on her own life, addressed the negative implications of the stages. After suffering from multiple strokes and residing in a bedridden state, she related, "I have loved and lost, and I am so much more than five stages. And so are you. It is not just about knowing the stages."[29] The creator of the five stages, after traveling her

---

[29] Elisabeth Kübler-Ross and Daniel Kessler, *On Grief and Grieving* (New York: Scribner, 2005), 216.

own grief journey, concurred the stages indeed fell short. In her original analysis which prompted the creation of stages, she aimed to assist the dying not the grieving. Thus, there was unintentional transference placed onto grievers worldwide, for all time.

The first message people need to know to reform our ministry with those who are grieving is that grief is particular, contextual, and nonlinear. The suggestion that grief should be on a spectrum is no doubt well-intended, but, as revealed, a well-established conundrum. We all suffer unto our own paradigms, in our fashions. As a man in his late twenties, Sam, who lost his young wife to cancer confessed, "Grief is highly personal. Absolutely no one has the same path." As stated in the opening journal entry, grief is never asked for. But as a part of life, it shows up on its own time, in its own way. In her book, *Anxiety: The Missing Stage of Grief,* psychologist Claire Bidwell Smith relates, "Grief-related anxiety is most often a result of trying to suppress or avoid the strong emotions that come with loss. As painful as they are, we must let them course through us. They're not going anywhere until they do. Grief has its own time line and its own plan for you."[30]

Second, on the journey through grief, compassion is a bona fide necessity for the griever. As pastoral theologian Carrie Doehring suggests, "Kindling compassion can in turn help care seekers reclaim or find new spiritual practices that bring solace and comfort, especially when grief is intense."[31] A new vision can become a griever's inspiration for the formidable task of daily moving-on, securing one foot in front of the other along treacherous emotional terrain. "Building such spiritual practices into daily life can help establish a rhythm more likely to sustain

---

[30] Claire Bidwell Smith, *Anxiety: The Missing Stage of Grief* (New York: Hachette, 2018), 49.

[31] Carrie Doehring, *The Practice of Pastoral Care* (Louisville: Westminster John Knox, 2015), 125.

a sense of the goodness of life throughout the day."[32] That being said, the duty lies on the griever to locate and implement such practices. If a counselor, pastor or chaplain is there to assist the individual, they can direct the griever to potentially helpful practices. There may be local support groups and recommended readings to offer. Oftentimes just locating the internal initiative to connect to anything is taxing, albeit a likely helpful venture. For one immersed inside a cavern of grief, just making that move from their safe comfort zone into such an unknown scenario like a support group can be anxiety-producing. When I did finally force myself to make the call to visit a support group, my sadness was actually compounded as I was the only griever in my age bracket, the lone non-elderly representative. It was a cold winter's evening, and not only in the outdoor atmosphere. For some, groups and/or intensive counseling are a rock to stand upon. For others, a great deal of time spent in nature is the ultimate balm of healing. Still for others a community—whether church parishioners or close friends—provides foundational roots. The answer rests only with the griever.

Third, the fruitful practice of meaning-making can also have profound positive effects. Such is a component of a prominent hospice community in Nashville. Alive Hospice sponsors a summer camp for children who have lost close loved ones. Activities include creating posters with characteristics and drawings, and painting souvenir boxes for mementos. Tangible objects help to connect to the loss. Similarly, placing photographs of the deceased around the house helps keep memories alive. As painful as it is to be reminded daily of the loss, the presence of tangible objects helps fuse the lifelong presence of heart connection. To be reminded often that love never dies is a powerful concept. By keeping such sacred items in the immediate environment, a provision is made for instilling

---

[32] Ibid., 125.

memories. A sanctuary of remembrances is a healing, ritualized space that is pragmatic in nature.

Finally, caregivers can invite a "search in the soul" or a trust or reliance on forces, divine and otherwise, beyond ourselves. While all of these examples of healing assistance are sincere and honorable in nature, they may be beyond the griever's reach. This is precisely where one's higher power and clarity can intervene, into the individual's own journey. If grief is incapable of systemic stages, then grief is capable of its own flow. Let's give the grieving process back to grief and the griever. The search into the soul is the only dimension where authentic healing can be birthed. Nothing looks the same after loss. The light that once streamed through the window with a cheery glow is now blinding. Only the griever can attest to what specific components have revived their sense of hope. The long walk through the shadows ends in a field of daylight only when the griever is able to grasp that light.

journal

⟋𝓂⟍

I don't know what Charlie Brown was referring to when he so frequently stated "good grief." I'm face-deep in the black, soily muck of so-called grief and none of it is "good." I thought being a divorced, infertile with septuple miscarriages woman would be the worst of my life, but oh, how wrong I was. Eight weeks ago my sweet husband left this world right in front of me, with our four-year-old son upstairs obediently staying put in his room. There aren't words that have been created to accurately describe grief.

Grief is ghastly. It must have the same likeness and characteristics of the bottom rim of an eternal pit. I say "anguish" but that sounds way too light. I say "sorrow" and that doesn't even cut to the edge of the truth. Grief is the worst feeling imaginable. Why? Because you can't do anything about it. You just have to sit with it. You can't eat enough, shop enough, travel enough, drink enough, medicate enough, exercise enough, or pray enough. It never goes anywhere but stays brick-wall-thick plopped right into the core of your heart. And it ain't going anywhere fast. Grief isn't nice. It doesn't ask to come or to go away. It doesn't care what you think or feel or need or want. You cannot outrun it, undercut it, or ignore it. Grief is just mean. And no one ever asks for it. Yet it shows up, right on its own time, slashing through souls.

Do I believe in God? Yes. Do I understand God who allows 4-year-olds' daddies to die unexpectedly? No. I unequivocally without hesitation will say I do not understand that God. Does it make me question God? Yes. Does it make me even doubt His existence? Yes. Does the whole "we live in a fallen world" and "Adam and Eve ate the apple" solve my pain or ease my grief? *No*, a resounding no. I'm not the least concerned about apples eaten centuries ago or fallen worlds or theology or any talk about anything, period. I just want my husband and my son's father here with us. And now that cannot be. A little forewarning would've been helpful. A diagnosis, a potential knowing that something like this could happen might have at least prepared us. But no. This death tsunami just rolled in through this house Sunday afternoon with zero warning. What do I make of such horrific tragedy? I never dreamt something so terrible could happen.

If you're hoping this ends on a more positive note, I'm afraid I've failed you. I am in continual intensive therapy and support groups to deal with the aftermath of feelings and just ground-zero pain. I have no answers. I have no beautiful C.S. Lewis-esque gorgeous literary writings of grief. I have this: two parts of anger, one part sadness, and another part of utter confusion. Friends have mentioned to me the goodness of God, but I will be heartfelt and honest and say that thought shocks me instantly. I'm pretty mad at him. Little boys' fathers shouldn't be taken away. Period.

So no ... right now I don't have any redemptive stories of how blessed we are or how grateful I am or any Pollyanna-ish junk. We have been sliced and now live each day with a mortal wound. Maybe one day, maybe far away, I will have different eyes to see, different glasses with which to view this experience. But I know this much: grief is real, grief comes to every person at some point, and grief can't be encapsulated and explained away with an easy-breezy response.

Cassidy's Experience

⌒*⌒*

Dealing with the guilt experienced due to an unexpected—or maybe even expected—loss. The head often knows there's nothing you could have done or changed, but the heart doesn't listen to the head! That was the hardest part of dealing with the loss of our son for us. I carried tremendous guilt even though it was irrational.

Deborah's Experience

The most painful grief I have felt is grieving the living. I had to end a long-term friendship because of an ongoing behavior. We were fast friends. We were thick as thieves. I confided in her and she in me. So as you can assume, it broke my heart that this person whom I loved so much and who I thought was my best friend was someone I truly didn't know at all. My heart was broken, and yes, I grieved the loss of our friendship, but also I rejoiced in the fact that chapter was closed in my life. I miss her every day, but some friends aren't in your life forever. As my friend Rachel's mom said, "When you become an adult, if you can count on one hand the number of TRUE friends you have then you are a lucky person." But I will tell you that even though I grieve my friendship with her, I have felt free knowing that I'm living a more wholesome life.

Taylor's Experience

Grief and guilt went hand in hand for me. I always felt like I had done something "wrong" or had disappointed people (family in particular). Like any process, it gets better with time. I now look back on my life with such gratefulness and humbleness. Every once in a while I still grieve for what could have been or what I thought my life should have been. But nowadays I pay attention to little things—signs from people who have passed on that I was close to or loved. Now when I get those signs I am grateful and usually say out loud that I got the sign they were sending loud and clear. My grief has *finally* turned to gratitude.

Kimberly's Experience

In my circumstance, it has been very difficult for me to accept the permanence of my son's disability. While he is very much here, loved, and a part of our family, I often find myself grieving milestones that other children hit at a given age. For example, he was never able to play T-ball like I did, or be in a typical kindergarten class. He doesn't really have friends other than his sister, and at least to this point, we have never had a lengthy reciprocal conversation. Losses can be experienced even when one is physically present, and we grieve "what could have been."

Ken's Experience

I haven't had any significant grief from deaths of others, but I have real, ongoing pain grieving loved ones still alive. There is an estrangement within my family that has really taken its toll. It sent me into a severe depression, which I went to an inpatient hospital for. I could not get past the fact my own family disowned me. It broke my heart. Grief for living people is really hard. It seems like it should be able to be fixed, but in my case, it's not reality.

Sarah's Experience

Since I was three, I have wanted to be a ballerina. When I started elementary school, my parents had me enrolled in dance classes after school, which I just loved! My teacher, Mrs. Yvette, said I was a natural and that I was going places. I didn't know what that meant at such a young age, but her support gave me confidence. All throughout my growing up years, I danced. I joined a troupe and we traveled around our region for many summers. With this being such a strong-suited fit for me since I was a toddler, I assumed that would be my career. It was always at the forefront of my mind that I would "make it." I was accepted into a prestigious college in the Northeast and spent four years honing my skills and craft. I even danced on Broadway in several productions. But then the auditions came to a screeching halt. I waited tables, hoping against all hope that I would dance again.

One year became two, became three. Sure, I danced in my little studio apartment just for myself, for the sheer pleasure and personal joy, but the day came when I realized the hard truth it wouldn't be the career I had dreamed of. This was a hard pill. I found a great counselor, Peggy, who showed me the wide world of options at my fingertips. I had so honed in on being a star ballerina that I hadn't thought of what else was out there. I found a dance studio looking for part-time help with young children. They hired me on the spot, and for five years now I have been training the next generation of ballerinas. But the grief of letting go of that lifelong dream was as painful as anything I can think of. My identity was in this dream that didn't happen. It was a deep, deep loss and the only thing that eased the pain was helping those little kids. Sometimes I still feel the grief over the dream not coming true, like an old familiar feeling in my gut.

Elliott's Experience

In the span of two months, I lost both of my parents to COVID-19. The anguish and pain of these losses ... well, I will never emotionally recover. It was all so sudden. It literally felt like we were hugging one day, then they fell ill the next. The nurses and chaplains gave their all, helping me to at least see mom and dad through the tiny square windows. But it just hurt, and it still hurts. I feel like I'm walking around the world like a zombie. Part of me wants everyone I see to know what happened so they will take this virus more seriously. Another part of me doesn't want anyone's sympathy. Then still another part just wants to go lie in a hole somewhere dark and not come out. How will I ever get to the other side of this? Happiness seems so out of reach.

part three

daffodils

But see, today is sunny. There is hope *this day*, and spring shooting forth on buttercup heads, and a bright bulbous sun laughing on my hair. It's what I think they call, a better day. I stopped in our favorite burger place to have our favorite lunch with our favorite beer. The table-for-one scenario is tiring, and old, and boring, and sad still. No Pollyanna here, no Sir, not even with floral optimism bounding round every patch of grass. I wish to God—literally—you were here, on your lunch break, meeting me for a quick bite. We'd laugh about some funny thing our son said yesterday at the movie, when the Marvin Gaye song came on and he asked, "Is that Steve Harvey singing?" We'd be all smiles and jokes. Not that all our days were smiles and jokes ... but this one would be. Because we would now know what we didn't before. That our relationship won't last forever, or for even old age. That you'd be gone in a camera flash, with a wake so high it sunk nearly all of us. We would laugh and smile and joke because we would know then that life is incredibly short and we have little control over that hard fact.

Look at that couple with the baby ... she looks angry ... eyes darting away and then glaring again at him while she feeds the baby green peas. The guy's on his phone this entire time. Don't they know? Don't they know all they have can be upended with one cardiac arrest? We all take each other for granted; I think no one is immune, certainly not myself. We all get into a rhythm and forget the beat can stop at any time. A normal Sunday can be the end of someone's life. Fact news, not fake news. Ask me how I know ... actually, don't.

I find myself wanting to announce to every dining room, every airport gate, every church group, every place people are gathered that we all need to *wake up and realize people can be gone in a second*. You know, I honestly thought everyone grew old and died in their eighties or nineties. I was served up this putrid theology promising us a minimum of eighty years because of some verse in the Bible. Now that right there, is fake news. This life is the most unpredictable and precarious endeavor we could ever embark upon. It's a wonder we do it. I'm gonna run now. I may pick a buttercup from the nearby sidewalk selection and indulge myself in a sensory immersion of yellow springs. And today, Dave, is a sun-lit beaming world of yellow! The sky is pristine, save for the one white, foamy X created by airplanes, which Jude and I say is a sign from you. The daffodils are screaming out in delight. We looked out the sunroof and saw the giant white X that says you are there watching over us.

a child's view of grief

Grief comes and goes, but it will always stay, in a way. It might seem confusing, but I'll explain. It's kinda simple. So, what I mean is, you will always miss the lost, but there's always a way to get through it. It might be hard or it might be easy. It will always stay, but it might not seem like it. Don't be afraid of grief, it will never ever win. So, always believe in yourself no matter what.

- JUDE, AGE TEN

my nowadays

My nowadays are sunny, penny-copper-shiny in the sun days. I absolutely carry him and the loss, the underground mountain of grief inside of me. I walk with a bit more certainty I won't tumble and fall. My way of walking through the world has dramatically shifted. I currently hold the hand of a sixth-grader who exudes with compassion and complete love for everything good. I wouldn't say the struggle is over, because we will always miss David. We are fortunate to have a husband and father today in our life who understands this. He knows he's here to show up for where we are now.

I'm coming at you from the "back 40" of grief. I'm blissfully wed to my best friend, a cute guy I liked many moons ago in our college days. I've read some of the grief journals, and my first thought was, "Whoa. That writer (me) sounds legit depressed." Then my following thought went something like, "How did that person raise a child and acquire a master's degree with that monsoon of anguish going on inside her?" And quite honestly, I have no idea. I was hurting deeply, and deeply hurt.

So, how did I reach the proverbial end of the line of active grief, you ask? Time and God in a long collaborative tandem. And love. And a cannonball splash of surrender. Topped and draped with grace. It's been six years, nine months.

Many times I feel like I've drifted through a fog and missed many moments due to reflection trapping. What I mean by that is getting lost in thoughts of what was, what could have been, what was not to be. I hope my son hasn't felt me zone out at times doing this, but likely he has. Sometimes I see photos of him from kindergarten, first grade, and it's like I can't recall those tender times whilst locked in the grief-cyclone.

Wishing I'd done better is futile as I did the best I could at the time, this I know. There are pictures of his dad all over his room, and sometimes he still cries missing him. I understand. Yet the new season is here, the sun is upon us. We spend our current days basking in yellow warmth.

You see, one overcast day last November, I had a big, fancy, aloud, matter-of-fact talk with God in the kitchen. I actually did it ... I surrendered. I gave up my wishing and wanting, trying to make things happen the way I thought I needed them to. I emotionally, spiritually, and physically let go, literally placing my hands in the air in the middle of a random weekday. I said, "God, I quit." I had spent a losing battle chasing one who couldn't love me or my son with anything because he himself was empty and emotionally void. I. Quit.

I'd always heard that, what I deemed cliché, "Let Go and Let God." But this time I really went for that. I threw in at the end of this ongoing prayer, that if God did in fact want me and Jude to have a man come into our lives, that he be someone I already knew (preferably attended college with), and was raised with morals and values, maintaining stability and employment. I even threw in golfer and Alabama football fan as I knew Jude would like that. Three days later, this guy crossed my mind. I hadn't seen or heard anything out of him in six years. I found him on Facebook, and sent him a message. "Hey Lew. Do you have a girlfriend?" I just went for it, no holds barred. And that was it. We were engaged two months later, married three months after that in a pandemic wedding. I reread those last words and still cannot believe it. All that has happened is mind-blowing.

A simple heartfelt prayer ... and lo and behold, he was there. Lewis is wise, wonderful, caring, and devoted. He is all the things

I asked God for. He adores my son and me, never raises his voice, is continually gentle and sincere. He's a calming force. He's exactly the man I described in my fervent kitchen prayer. Occasionally I've paused asking, "Is this too good to be true?" But it turns out, he's really just that good. Thank God.

Lewis was instantly family and he wanted to be with us. That changed everything in my broken heart. And now my son, in addition to his dad, had a had a superb example of how to be a man—a good, solid man. What I think "did it" was I surrendered totally, unequivocally. I let go … and let God. And God showed up big-time, more than I could've even imagined. Lewis checked off every single box I had requested. The act of surrender in turn set me free, but it took a really long time to reach that place. Nothing would heal me until I gave it up. Literally, up. Not that I don't think God is everywhere, because I do. It was more of a symbolic expression of lifting my surrender, as a noun, as an offering up to God. Very Old Testament-y, but it felt right and true. I wrote these words shortly after:

> Oh how long I wandered
> How long I cried
> The years I pondered
> will I make it out alive
> With just one message
> The wounds resolved
> I guess the lesson
> is trust in God

Once the surrender was fully enacted and the gift bestowed, more blessings ensued. Every positive occurrence that landed was another nod of "yes" to the path of goodness. My husband said our light would spread, and spread it did. The local paper covered our wedding, complete with an on-site photographer. Our story even bumped off the latest coronavirus data one day and made it to the top of the online page. Love does indeed spread, and the contagion we were faced with in the time of COVID-19, was nothing compared to the contagious activity of positivity. People needed good news, perhaps then more than ever. People needed love, and to see love does indeed win even in crises.

We hoped, and Lewis predicted, our love's light would touch others; we just had no clue that could reach over five hundred thousand people in the local newspaper in Nashville, Tennessee. Part of that light was how to help others struggling in the pandemic. We recognized our good fortune of being at home with our family, plenty of food, and time together. We also recognized many folks were on the frontlines risking their very lives to save others. So we thought that any money given us for a wedding gift would feed those brave, courageously gifted healthcare workers and janitorial crews. For the first few weeks post-wedding, we had the opportunity to serve such heroes a simple, hot meal. Maybe it wasn't much, but it was something … a small token of "thank you." The love light was spreading. Then we were given an advertising gift of $2,500 on a local website. Those monies provided meals for the frontline heroes as well. And the best part, in my opinion, was the ten dollars that would come in, the fifteen dollars that may have been all that donor could afford. The kindness of strangers made a big difference, no matter the amount. As of this writing, 178 frontline healthcare workers and janitors have been fed a hot meal thanks to the generosity of others. The next delivery will feed a crew of sixty-five at Vanderbilt University Medical Center. All of this is to say, the love light does indeed spread … even in a pandemic. Or maybe, especially in a pandemic, when we are all paying attention.

I penned this song for Lewis soon after we began dating. True story … "I asked God for a raindrop, He sent the flood."

| Raindrop |

My heart was fried, burned out love
Dog tired, I'd given up
Desert air, oasis none
I declared this girl is done

Laid on the ground, raised my hands
Asked the clouds, "do you understand?"
On a dime, he lifted me
The nick of time, a wellspring

Giving in ain't my style
He washed me clean with just a smile

No more desert sand
No more desert land
I've reached the water
Swimming in the water
My head is covered
Still I can sing somehow
In the water
Underneath the water
I asked God for a raindrop,
He sent the flood

Take my word, gonna be ok
Even on sun-scorched days
Hold your faith like a stone
You are never alone

Surrendering
changes everything

No more desert sand
No more desert land
I've reached the water
Swimming in the water
My head is covered
Still I can sing somehow
In the water
Underneath the water
I asked God for a raindrop,
He sent the flood
Yeah I asked God for a raindrop
Just one little raindrop
A girl's simple prayer
Then you were there

No more desert sand
No more desert land
I've reached the water
Living in the water
My head is covered
Still I can sing somehow
In the water
Underneath the water
I asked God for a raindrop,
just one little raindrop
Yeah I asked God for a raindrop
He sent the flood

https://www.youtube.com/watch?v=DjrhGFb_eec

closing thoughts

Grief and faith are strange bedfellows. Grief asks, "Why faith?" Faith asks, "Why grief?" It is not uncommon for people to lose their faith after loss. I myself have waded in such waters and know the precise pull of the current. Sense-making in the wake of death is difficult. The conglomerate of emotions is a mixed bag. And none of your feelings regarding grief are wrong or bad, no matter what you've heard otherwise. Remember those trying to help with unfortunate messages are often captive within ingrained theologies and dogmatic thought processes. You are free to feel however you feel. I hope this is comforting news. Authenticity breeds strength, and expressing your feelings is a healthy space.

If you're like me, you might receive a clinical mental health diagnosis. Thankfully, there are medicines and therapists who can help. Remember if you were a diabetic, a prescription for insulin would be given. If you had high cholesterol, a statin would be prescribed. Both of these are used to correct imbalances in your body. Well, your body has a brain. It too can have imbalances. Mental health issues are medical. There are amazing medicines that alleviate your pain. I promise you that your situation—no matter how dire it seems—can be helped. As my mom says, "There is always an answer. You just have to keep looking." Keep searching high and low until you find the solution that works for you.

No, you most certainly didn't ask for death and grief to show up so haphazardly, and you definitely didn't summon the grim reaper. But you *can* get through it. I would not say these words if they weren't true; I have lived it. Believe. And even if you've lost your faith in God, have faith in your personal grit and fortitude to carry you into your best self, your best life beyond grief. Please do not feel afraid, embarrassed, or ashamed to find solutions that work for you. You've been through enough; shame is the last thing you need. And feel freedom to share that sentiment with those who are expressing their misguided care and love in unfruitful, unproductive, and unhelpful ways. Who knows? You may teach them compassion and empathy.

Know this, dear reader. You are already on your way. The blinders will come up again, and you will see the bluebird sky, the summer-green grass, and cheery daffodils.

reader reflections

What is the first thing that comes to your mind when you hear the word "grief?"

_____

_____

_____

_____

_____

_____

How do you see grief represented in your culture?

_____

_____

_____

_____

_____

_____

Have you experienced a painful reaction from another person while expressing your own grief? What was said or done?

_____

_____

_____

_____

_____

_____

_____

What do you wish this person had said or done differently?

_____

_____

_____

_____

_____

_____

_____

_____

Do you relate to any of the experiences expressed?

_____

_____

_____

_____

_____

_____

_____

Have you ever felt pressure to work the grief-staging process?

_____

_____

_____

_____

_____

_____

_____

_____

Have you experienced grief in a manner not mentioned in this book? If so, what does that look like for you?

_____

_____

_____

_____

_____

_____

_____

_____

If you engage in spirituality and/or religion, how has your life in this area been impacted by the experience of grief?

_____

_____

_____

_____

_____

_____

_____

_____

_____

Considering the well-known grief stages, have you found that approach to be effective or helpful in your grief journey?

_____

_____

_____

_____

_____

_____

_____

_____

Is there an aspect of grief you have experienced that feels unique to you? A characteristic you feel that is yet to be addressed?

_____

_____

_____

_____

_____

_____

_____

_____

_____

bibliography

Barber, Betsy. "Grieving Like God," The Good Book (blog). October 24, 2017. Accessed October 12, 2019. https://www.biola.edu/blogs/good-book-blog/2017/grieving-like-god.

Coble, Richard. *The Chaplain's Presence and Medical Power.* Maryland: Lexington, 2018.

Doehring, Carrie. *The Practice of Pastoral Care.* Louisville: Westminster John Knox, 2006.

Kübler-Ross, Elisabeth. *On Death and Dying.* New York: Simon & Schuster, 1969.

Kübler-Ross, Elisabeth and David Kessler. *On Grief and Grieving.* New York: Scribner, 2005.

Lewis, C.S. *A Grief Observed.* New York: HarperCollins, 1996.

Mead, Frank. *Who's Who in the Bible.* New York: Harper & Bros., 1934.

Miller-McLemore, Bonnie. *Death, Sin and the Moral Life.* Atlanta: Scholars, 1988.

Mitchell, Kenneth R. and Anderson, Herbert. *All Our Losses, All Our Griefs*. Louisville: Westminster John Knox, 1983.

Smith, Claire Bidwell. *Anxiety: The Missing Stage of Grief.* New York: Hachette, 2018.

Stroebe, Margaret, Henk Schut, and Kathrin Boerner. "Cautioning Health-Care Professionals: Bereaved Persons Are Misguided Through the Stages of Grief." *OMEGA* 74 (2017): 455-473. https://journals.sagepub.com/doi/pdf/10.1177/0030222817691870 (accessed October 14, 2019).

Tatelbaum, Judy. *The Courage to Grieve*. New York: HarperCollins, 1980.

Printed in the United States
by Baker & Taylor Publisher Services